T0194242

Copyright © 2023 by Shaun Gill and Dr. Tamara Clark.

ISBN: Softcover   978-1-6698-6213-0
               eBook   978-1-6698-6212-3

All rights reserved. No part of this book may be reproduced or transmitted in any form or by any means, electronic or mechanical, including photocopying, recording, or by any information storage and retrieval system, without permission in writing from the copyright owner.

Any people depicted in stock imagery provided by Getty Images are models, and such images are being used for illustrative purposes only.
Certain stock imagery © Getty Images.

Print information available on the last page.

Rev. date: 01/05/2023

To order additional copies of this book, contact:
Xlibris
844-714-8691
www.Xlibris.com
Orders@Xlibris.com
849979

Activities for Every Season
ACTIVITY BOOK FOR KIDS

Written by:
Shaun Gill and
Tamara Clark – Gill, Phd

Illustrated by:
Jenevie Valdehueza

COPYRIGHT 2023

Activities For Every Season

During Bill's journey, he always
bring a toy to create memories along
with the family and friends.
He lives in the part of the world that allows
him to experience all 4 seasons; Winter,
Spring, Summer and Fall.
Let's create memories with Bill!

Winter Season

Bill's Favorite Activity in the Winter

Baking with Mom

Bill loves to bake items such as, cookies, muffins, and cakes with his mom. His favorite items to bake are chocolate chip cookies, muffins and chocolate cakes.

Bill's mom loves for him to help her while baking, because it helps him

- Follow instructions.

- Learn about measurements.

- Exercise patience while baking.

- Increase interest of cooking and baking.

Bill's Toy of Choice

During the cold weather, Bill plays cards with family members and friends. The box of cards allow Bill to learn in many ways. Let's see!

WORD SCRAMBLE

How does the card game help Bill?

1. The card game can help Bill have
   __ _u_ __ with others.

2. The card game can help Bill follow
   _ _i_ _ _ _c_ _i_ _ _ _s_ .

3. The card game can help Bill with
   _ _ _m_ _ _e_ _ _s_ .

Bill is preparing for the cold weather. The winter weather can be very cold and snow can accumulate during the season.

Please help Bill prepare for the cold winter season. What items do Bill need to stay warm at home and school?

Please help Bill figure out what he needs to prepare for the winter season.

1. _ l _ v _ s

2. C _ _ t

3. B _ _ _ _ s

4. _ w _ _ t _ r

5. _ a _

6. _ _ t _ e _ s

7. _ c _ r _

WORD SCRAMBLE

Please create words using the phrase shown below.

Bill Toy Box Adventures

1. _____
2. _____
3. _____
4. _____
5. _____
6. _____
7. _____
8. _____
9. _____
10. _____

11. _____
12. _____
13. _____
14. _____
15. _____
16. _____
17. _____
18. _____
19. _____

WORDS TO SEARCH

gloves   sweater   scarf   boots

coat   hat   mittens

d	w	a	f	t	n	o	f	b	c	a
v	z	f	a	k	i	b	o	n	j	d
q	s	i	d	g	z	o	k	m	s	d
e	o	y	f	l	d	o	i	s	k	j
u	s	k	c	o	a	t	o	p	d	s
c	e	j	o	v	t	s	u	h	g	c
g	j	l	f	e	o	p	d	a	l	a
k	i	l	n	s	w	e	a	t	e	r
p	t	s	f	g	u	m	b	d	e	f
l	k	m	z	y	a	g	j	k	l	h

Tic Tac Toe
Break

Play with a friend or relative

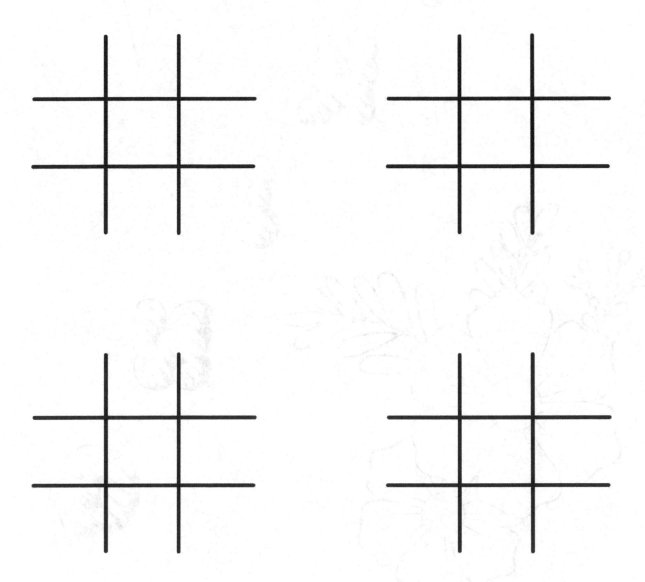

Spring Season

Bill loves to see the changes in the environment from cold to warm weather. He does not have to wear a big coat, scarf and hat for now. Instead, Bill can wear a jacket, a shirt and a pair of pants. Sometimes, the weather is warm enough to wear a shirt and a pair of pants.

Color a Page

Bill's favorite
Activities in the Spring

During the spring season, Bill visits the zoo to see all of the wonderful and exotic animals. Let's identify the animals during his trips at the zoo.

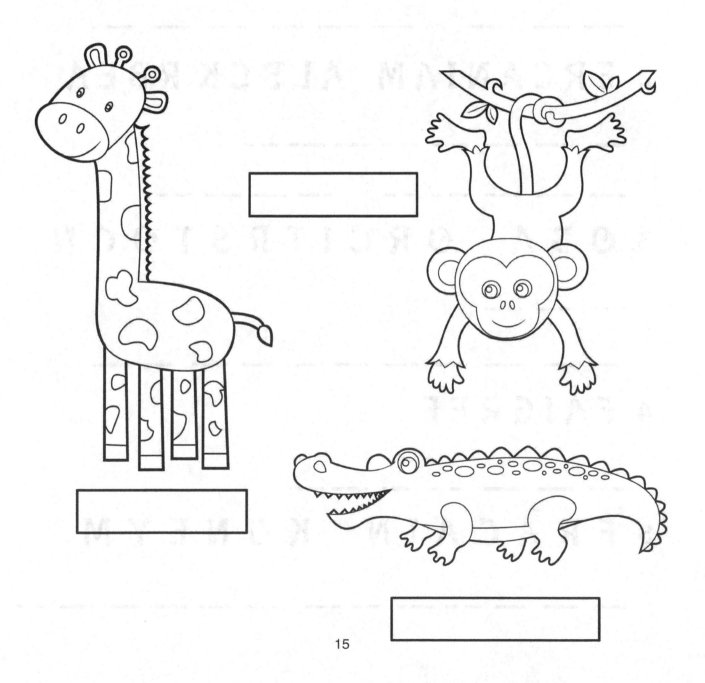

Please help Bill identify additional exotic animals at the zoo.

1. A S E   E U L T T R

_ _ _ _   _ _ _ _ _ _ _

2. E R C A N I A M   A L B C K R B E A

_ _ _ _ _ _ _ _

_ _ _ _   _ _ _ _ _

3. O B A   O R C I T R S T O C N

_ _ _

_ _ _ _ _ _ _ _ _ _ _

4. F A I G R E F

_ _ _ _ _ _ _ _

5. F R A C A I N   K O N E Y M

_ _ _ _ _ _ _   _ _ _ _ _ _

Words to Search

Cow   Camel   Rabbit
Sting ray   Sheep   Bison   Turtle
Horse   Flamingo   Snake

a	c	z	i	e	g	h	f	m	b
w	f	b	c	a	m	e	l	i	o
o	s	p	j	z	y	d	a	f	l
c	t	n	g	y	z	d	m	e	t
e	i	d	a	f	s	g	i	r	q
l	n	c	a	k	h	j	n	a	n
t	g	o	s	q	e	t	g	b	o
r	r	w	n	j	e	k	o	b	s
u	a	o	j	p	p	y	x	i	i
t	y	h	o	r	s	e	a	t	b

Bill's Toy of Choice
Plastic Garden Tools

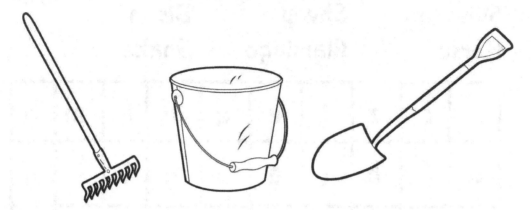

These favorite tools are used when Bill and his mother begins to garden. Bill works very close with his mother to plant flowers, vegetables, and fruit in the garden.

Can you help Bill identify some plants to grow?

Vegetables and fruits to plant this year

1. __C__ __ __b__ __ __ __g__ __e__

2. __S__ __ __ __ __ __ __
   __ __ __a__ __s__

3. __ __a__ __ __r__ __t__ __

4. __B__ __ __ __l__ __ __
   __P__ __ __ __ __ __r__ __

5. __ __e__ __b__ __t__ __c__ __

6. S _ _ _ _ b _ _ _ i _ s

7. _ P _ l _ _ _

8. P _ _ c _ e _

9. _ o _ a _ o _ _

10. R _ _ i _ _ e _

What items are needed for Bill and his mom to begin gardening?

Bill needs tools such as a

_ a k _ , s h _ v _ l ,
b _ c k _ t , and _ i _ t
to name a few. Bills needs s _ e d _
and flower pots. Also, Bill can make room in the backyard to plant

f l _ w _ r _ ,
f _ _ u _ t , and
v _ g _ t _ b l e s .

After Bills plant everything, he needs to

w a _ _ r them as needed. Also he needs to made sure all of them receives

s u _ l _ g h t to grow.

Words to Search

Water   Sunlight   Flower

Seed   Rake   Bucket   Vegetables

Shovel   Fruit   Garden

a	d	d	c	e	z	y	l	i	k	j	b
z	o	k	l	p	l	j	w	c	d	f	v
o	j	k	z	x	r	w	a	c	e	j	e
n	l	b	u	c	k	e	t	x	r	o	g
e	p	o	w	k	s	e	e	d	q	s	a
d	a	c	j	k	h	i	r	s	f	x	t
r	s	x	f	l	o	w	e	r	r	j	a
a	o	d	x	f	v	j	p	t	u	k	b
g	a	r	a	k	e	b	x	c	i	b	l
v	w	s	u	n	l	i	g	h	t	k	e
l	e	f	x	d	n	w	k	f	o	p	s

Tic Tac Toe
Break
Play with a friend or relative

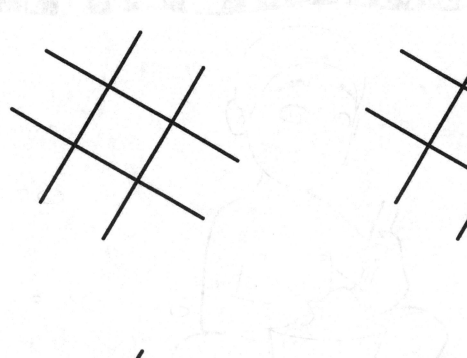

SUMMER TIME

24

BiLL's Favorite
Activity in the Summer

UACATION TIME

Bill is going camping with his parents!

Please help Bill with the items needed for his trip!

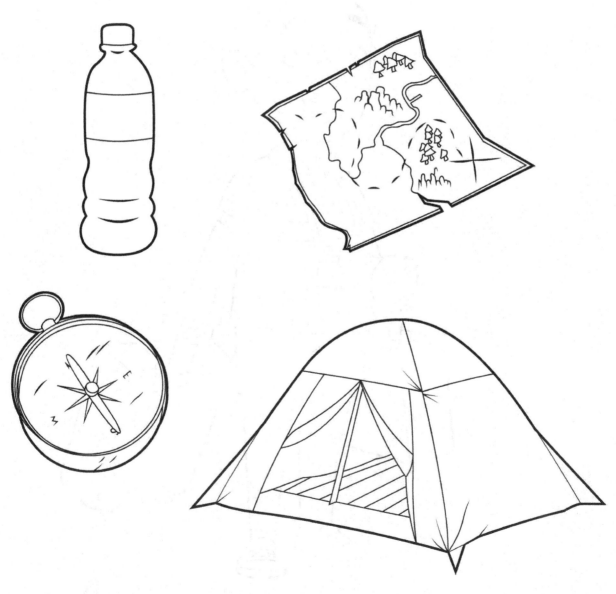

What are the essential items needed to go camping?

1. __t__ __ __ __ __ __t__

2. __ __l__ __ __ __h__
   __ __ __ __h__ __

3. __S__ __ __ __ __P__ __ __g__
   __ __a__ __

4. <u>f</u> __ <u>r</u> __ __ <u>t</u>
   __ <u>i</u> __ <u>k</u> __ <u>t</u>

5. <u>P</u> __ <u>c</u> __ __ <u>t</u>
   <u>k</u> __ <u>l</u> __ <u>c</u>

6. __ <u>o</u> __ __ __ __ <u>s</u>

7. <u>r</u> __ <u>i</u> __ <u>c</u> __ <u>a</u> __

8. <u>w</u> __ __ <u>r</u>
   __ <u>o</u> <u>t</u> __ __ __

9. c __ __ p

__ __ __ i __

10. m __ t __ h __ s

What activities can Bill do while camping with his family?

1. Bike riding

2. Make simores for dessert

3. Play board games

4. Create scary stories

5. Complete scavenger hunt

6. Hiking

7. Play cards

8. Read books

What activities do you play with your family?

1. _____

2. _____

3. _____

31

Where do you go on vacation?

Where do you go on vacation?
Please write four (4) places to go on vacation.

1. _____

2. _____

3. _____

4. _____

Word Scramble

Bill is traveling to a beach to have fun in the sun. Please help Bill with various items that he needs to take with him.

1. <u>n</u> <u>d</u> <u>a</u> <u>s</u>
   <u>e</u> <u>u</u> <u>c</u> <u>b</u> <u>k</u> <u>t</u>

   _ _ _ _

   _ _ _ _ _ _

2. <u>e</u> <u>l</u> <u>o</u> <u>v</u> <u>h</u> <u>s</u>

   _ _ _ _ _ _

3. <u>n</u> <u>s</u> <u>u</u> <u>c</u> <u>e</u> <u>r</u> <u>e</u> <u>s</u>

   <u>n</u> <u>o</u> <u>t</u> <u>l</u> <u>i</u> <u>o</u>

   _ _ _ _ _ _ _ _ _

   _ _ _ _ _ _ _

4. <u>n</u> <u>s</u> <u>u</u>

   <u>l</u> <u>g</u> <u>s</u> <u>e</u> <u>a</u> <u>s</u> <u>s</u>

   _ _ _ _

   _ _ _ _ _ _

5. <u>c</u> <u>b</u> <u>a</u> <u>h</u> <u>e</u>

   <u>o</u> <u>e</u> <u>t</u> <u>w</u> <u>l</u>

   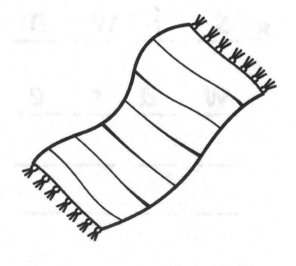

   _ _ _ _ _

   _ _ _ _ _

6. <u>p</u> <u>l</u> <u>i</u> <u>f</u>
   <u>s</u> <u>o</u> <u>p</u> <u>f</u> <u>l</u>

   _ _ _ _

   _ _ _ _ _

7. <u>c</u> <u>e</u> <u>a</u> <u>b</u> <u>h</u>
   <u>g</u> <u>b</u> <u>a</u>

   _ _ _ _ _

   _ _ _

8. <u>s</u> <u>i</u> <u>w</u> <u>m</u>
   <u>w</u> <u>a</u> <u>r</u> <u>e</u>

   _ _ _ _

   _ _ _ _

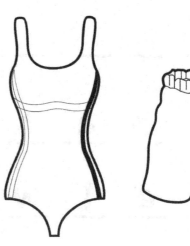

WORD SEARCH

water   play   swim suit   flip flops

sand   umbrella   towel   castle

summer   vacation

s	p	o	l	f	p	i	l	f	n
w	z	l	s	o	p	r	q	t	o
i	b	w	a	t	e	r	s	u	i
m	x	g	n	y	v	w	k	n	t
s	r	f	d	t	j	j	q	e	a
u	e	o	w	x	s	b	a	l	c
i	m	z	a	l	e	w	o	t	c
t	m	y	g	b	i	l	m	s	v
w	u	m	b	r	e	l	l	a	x
y	s	x	q	s	a	g	b	c	o

Extracurricular Activities

Bill's mom explore various interests by participating in various activities. For example, Bill has participated in

Basketball

Tennis

Wrestling

Soccer

Extracurricular Activities
During the Summer

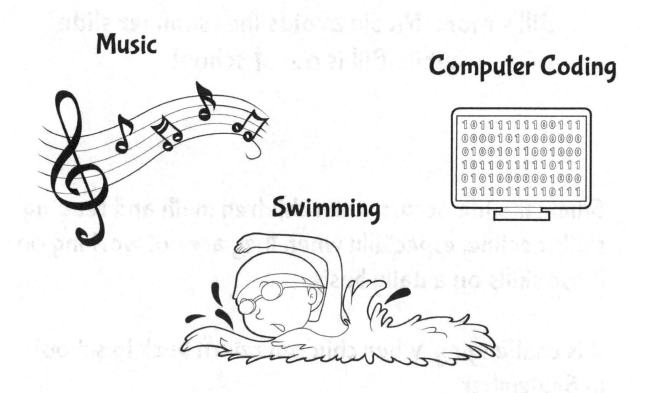

Music

Computer Coding

Swimming

Nicole has decided to register Bill to participate in the following activities shown above. Also, Bill continues to complete tutoring in Language Arts and Math to avoid summer slide.

Summer Slide

Bill's Mom, Nicole avoids the "summer slide" while Bill is out of school.

Summer slide occurs when children math and reading skills decline, especially when they are not working on those skills on a daily basis.

It is challenging, when children return back to school in September.

During the summer, it is important for children to
continue math, reading and writing skills
to avoid "summer slide" concerns.

Summer Slide
Tips

Bill's Mom, Nicole avoids the summer slide with small tips.

1. Schedule time to read a book with each other. It is important for Bill to select books that he is interested in.

2. Sacrifice and pay a tutor to provide support in math language arts.

3. Complete fun games or activities in computers, math and language arts to sharpen skills.

How do you avoid the "summer slide"?

1. _____

2. _____

3. _____

Tic Tac Toe
Break
Play with a friend or relative

Bill's favorite Activity in the Fall

Apple Picking

Bill loves going to local farms with his mom and friends. They are able to pick various types of fruit.

It allows everyone to
learn about different apples.
For example, there are McIntosh, Red
Delicious, Gala, Fugi, Honeycrisp
and Granny Smith to name a few.

Immediately after picking apples, they
enjoy drinking hot apple cider and
eating apple cider donuts together.

Bill loves to pick another popular fruit at the local farms. It is called a pumpkin.

Pumpkin picking in another activity that Bill loves to do. Before he select the pumpkin, Bill and friends have chance to go on a hay ride throughout the farm.

Color the page

Apple

Pumpkin

Bill's Toy of Choice

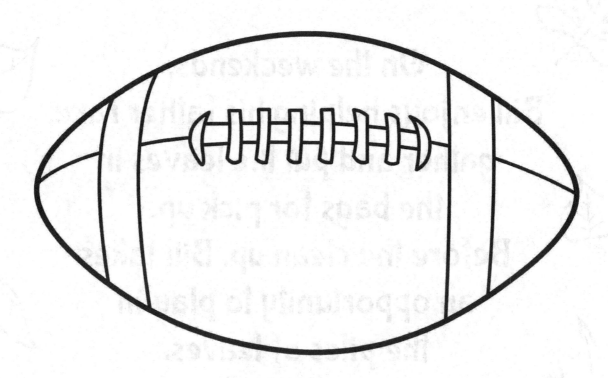

Football

Bill loves to play football with his family and friends. He loves to watch football with his father and uncle.

On the weekends,
Bill enjoys helping his father rake,
gather and put the leaves in
the bags for pick up.
Before the clean up, Bill takes
an opportunity to play in
the piles of leaves.

Word Scramble

What kind of physical activities are completed while raking leaves.

Children can complete the following activities:

1. <u>j</u> __ __ <u>p</u>

2. <u>r</u> __ <u>l</u> <u>l</u>

3. <u>p</u> __ __ <u>y</u>

4. _ l _ d _

5. r _ k _

6. c _ l l _ _ t

7. t _ r _ w

Color the page

Before Fall Season

During Fall Season

After Fall Season

Fall Season

September is here!

Bill needs to prepare for school. Please help Bill prepare for school. What does Bill's Mom, Nicole need to buy before school begin?

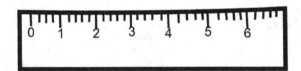

School Items
List

1. <u>r</u> <u> </u> <u> </u> <u>e</u> <u> </u>

2. <u>s</u> <u> </u> <u>i</u> <u> </u> <u> </u> <u>r</u> <u> </u>

3. <u>n</u> <u> </u> <u>e</u> <u> </u> <u> </u> <u>k</u>

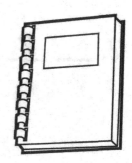

4. s __ __ __ k __ __ s

5. c __ __ t __ __ s

6. __ o l __ __ __ __

7. __ e __ __ __ __ s

8. <u>c</u> __ __ __ <u>y</u> __ __ <u>s</u>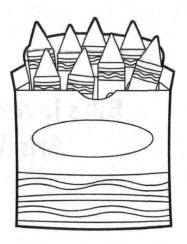

9. <u>b</u> __ __ __ __ <u>b</u> __ __

10. <u>l</u> __ <u>n</u> __ __ __ <u>o</u> __

59

All about School

Bill's favorite subjects are Math and Language Arts. What is your favorite subject in school?

_____ is my favorite subject in school.

Music

Science

Social Studies

Gym

Math

Writing

Language Arts

Bill's least favorite subject in school is
Social Studies. What is your least
favorite Subject ins school?

_____ is my least favorite subject
in school.

Writing

Music

Math

Gym

Science

Social Studies

WORD SEARCH

tool   pen   teacher   sack   shoe

school   pencil   sat   clock   cool

sock   book   lock   tock

a	c	b	j	k	s	s	f	d	l
t	o	o	l	p	t	a	r	o	o
a	t	c	q	s	o	c	k	z	o
f	g	l	j	m	o	z	f	z	h
h	z	o	l	n	l	o	q	y	c
s	a	c	k	j	t	o	c	k	s
z	p	k	y	f	h	i	a	l	p
g	l	o	p	e	n	c	i	l	b
h	o	z	s	a	t	l	p	f	o
n	c	j	p	t	c	o	o	l	o
e	k	t	y	s	h	o	e	y	k
p	r	e	h	c	a	e	t	d	r

Tic Tac Toe
Break
Play with a friend or relative

WORD SEARCH

tool pen teacher sack shoe
school pencil sat clock cool
sock book lock tock

a	c	b	j	k	s	s	f	d	l
t	o	o	l	p	t	a	r	o	o
a	t	c	q	s	o	c	k	z	o
f	g	l	j	m	o	z	f	z	h
h	z	o	l	n	l	o	q	y	c
s	a	c	k	j	t	o	c	k	s
z	p	k	y	f	h	i	a	l	p
g	l	o	p	e	n	c	i	l	b
h	o	z	s	a	t	l	p	f	o
n	c	j	p	t	c	o	o	l	o
e	k	t	y	s	h	o	e	y	k
p	r	e	h	c	a	e	t	d	r

Tic Tac Toe
Break
Play with a friend or relative

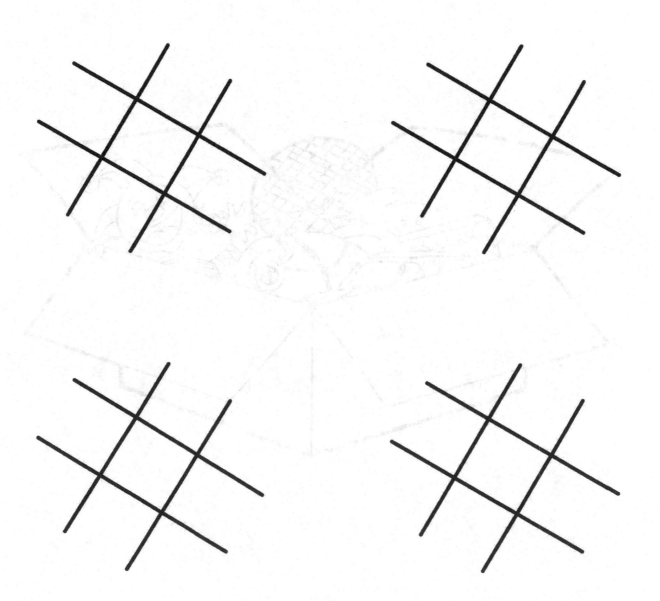

Thank you for having fun with Bill's favorite toys and activities.

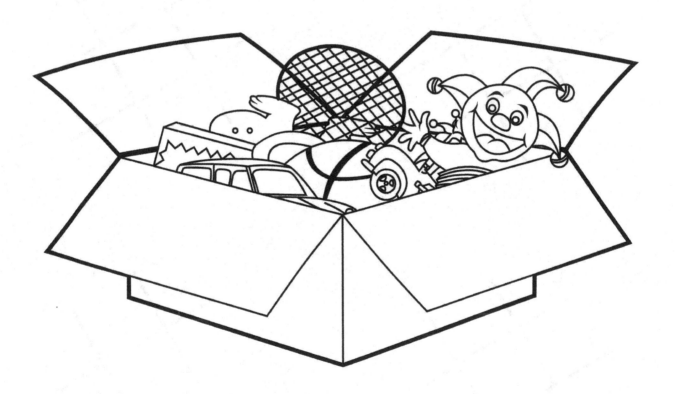

Winter Card Game
Answer key

1. fun

2. directions

3. numbers

Winter Season Items
Answer key

1. <u>g</u> <u>l</u> <u>o</u> <u>v</u> <u>e</u> <u>s</u>

2. <u>c</u> <u>o</u> <u>a</u> <u>t</u>

3. <u>b</u> <u>o</u> <u>o</u> <u>t</u> <u>s</u>

4. <u>s</u> <u>w</u> <u>e</u> <u>a</u> <u>t</u> <u>e</u> <u>r</u>

5. <u>h</u> <u>a</u> <u>t</u>

6. <u>m</u> <u>i</u> <u>t</u> <u>t</u> <u>e</u> <u>n</u> <u>s</u>

7. <u>s</u> <u>c</u> <u>a</u> <u>r</u> <u>f</u>

Word Scramble
Answer Key

1. toy
2. box
3. boy
4. ill
5. ox
6. venture
7. ant
8. at
9. vent
10. ad

11. tent
12. tray
13. lad
14. rent
15. sent
16. day
17. tent
18. nail
19. by

Exotic Zoo Animals
Answer key:

1. Sea Turtle

2. American Black Bear

3. Boa Constrictor

4. Giraffe

5. African Monkey

Vegetables and fruits to plant this year
Answer key:

1. Cabbage

2. String Beans

3. Carrots

4. Bell Pepper

5. Lettuce

6. Strawberries

7. Apples

8. Peaches

9. Tomatoes

10. Radishes

Gardening
Answer key:

1. rake

2. shovel

3. bucket

4. dirt

5. seeds

6. flowers

7. fruits

8. vegetables

9. water

10. sunlight

Camping
Answer key:

1. tent

2. flash light

3. sleeping bag

4. first aid kit

5. pocket knife

6. compass

7. rain coat

8. water bottle

9. camp chair

10. matches

Beach Word Scramble
Answer key:

1. Sand bucket

2. Shovel

3. Sunscreen lotion

4. Sun glasses

5. Beach towel

6. flip flops

7. Beach bag

8. Swim wear

Leaves Word Scramble
Answer key:

1. jump

2. roll

3. play

4. slide

5. rake

6. collect

7. throw

School Items
Answer key:

1. ruler

2. scissors

3. notebook

4. sneakers

5. clothes

6. folders

7. pencils

8. crayons

9. book bag

10. lunch box

Printed in the United States
by Baker & Taylor Publisher Services

Printed in the United States
by Baker & Taylor Publisher Services